This Book Belongs To:

Name _____

Phone _____

Email _____

Spooktacular

HALLOWEEN

MUSIC AND ACTIVITIES

Halloween-Themed Music Worksheets and Classroom
Activities with 10 Original Elementary Piano Compositions
for Singing or Playing

ISBN: 9798354997466

Table of Contents

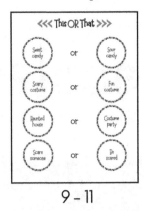

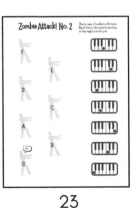

Table of Contents

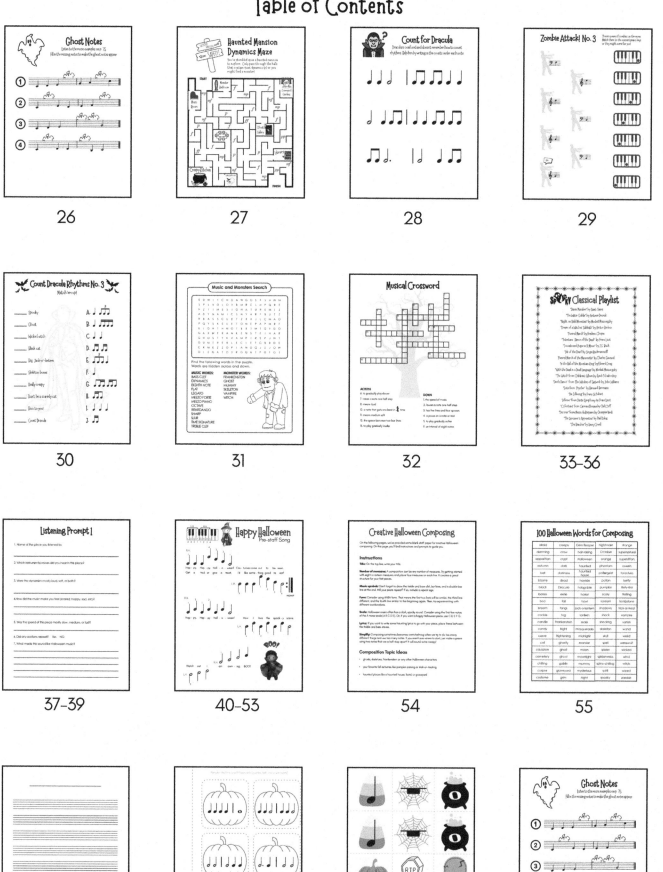

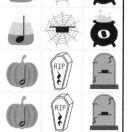

FORWARD

Spooktacular Halloween Music and Activities is designed to help reinforce important fundamentals for elementary musicians. There are plenty of leveled, elementary activities so you and your students can enjoy this resource for more than one year. Just pull it back out when the spooky season arrives, and you'll have more Halloween-themed activities waiting for you!

How to use this book:

- purchase individual copies of this book for music students to use during **private lessons**

- have fun with these activities at **music parties and group classes**

- use as supplementary worksheets for **elementary classroom** lesson plans

- enjoy this **one-stop, low-cost** activity book for 2-3 years or until students level up

- **cut down on time** finding and printing seasonal resources!

Want a digital download version of this book? Make lesson planning easy by purchasing a single-teacher digital license for these resources in our shop at creativepianoteacher.com.

Ghosts, ghouls, goblins.... oh my! A journey through Halloween music learning is here—are you ready to try?

The Creative Piano Teacher Team
Davis Dorrough and Dr. Olivia Ellis

WE NEED YOUR HELP!

We are a small business, and honest feedback and reviews from customers like you really make a difference. We would be honored if you would spread the word about our products by leaving a review on Amazon!

Halloween Music Jokes

What is a vampire's least favorite song?
You Are My Sunshine

What is a skeleton's favorite musical instrument?
A trom-bone

What are a mummy's two favorite kinds of music?
Wrap and ragtime

What happens if you play Beethoven backwards?
He decomposes

Why didn't the skeleton go to the dance?
He had no body to go with

Why did the vampire keep interrupting the piano recital?
Because of the coffin'

Why did the musician's gig at the graveyard go so badly?
The crowd was pretty dead

What kind of music do sad ghosts make?
Har – moan – y

Why was the vampire such a bad drummer?
He couldn't keep a steady pulse

Why were the musicians scared of the key of E minor?
It gave them the E-B-G-Bs

This OR That

What is This or That?

"This or That" is a game of preference where you get to show others what you like best. It's great to play as an icebreaker in groups and classes or as a solo activity with a friend, parent, or teacher. There's nothing that warms up a group more than discovering the things you have in common! In this edition of "This or That," we've put together some spooky topics to get you into the Halloween spirit.

Group Play Instructions

First, have everyone stand in a large room with enough space for the group to move around. Then, call out one of the "This or That" prompts on the following pages. For example, "would you rather eat sweet candy or sour candy?" Point to one side of the room as you say "sweet candy" and point to the other side as you say "sour candy." Instruct the group to quickly divide into two groups based on their individual preferences. That's it! Have fun getting to know others; the prompts highlight fun and sometimes strange features of your friends' personalities!

One-on-One Instructions

Go through the prompts and circle the ones that you like best. Share with a parent or teacher and find out which ones you have in common.

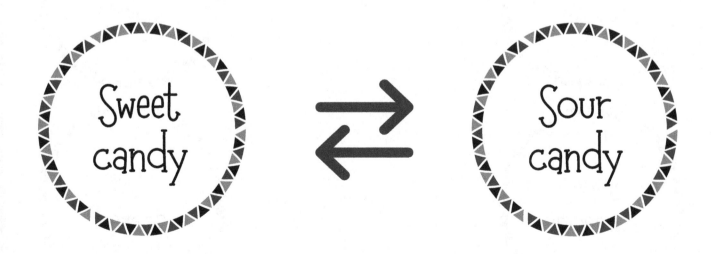

≪≪≪ This OR That ≫≫≫

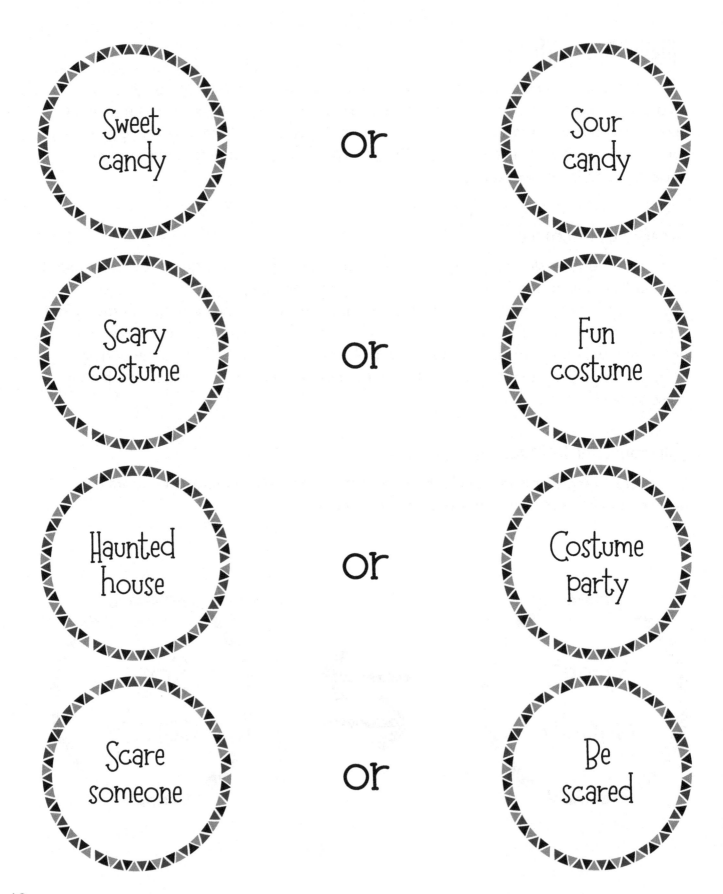

Sweet candy   or   Sour candy

Scary costume   or   Fun costume

Haunted house   or   Costume party

Scare someone   or   Be scared

10

This OR That

Buy a costume **or** Make a costume

Stay home and give out candy **or** Go trick or treating

Meet a vampire **or** Meet a werewolf

Carve 20 pumpkins **or** Eat 20 bags of candy corn

Right or Left?

A monster has left behind some spooky hand prints.
Write R on the right hands and L on the left hands.

Witch Hands Finger Numbers

Draw the correct finger number above each finger of this musical witch!

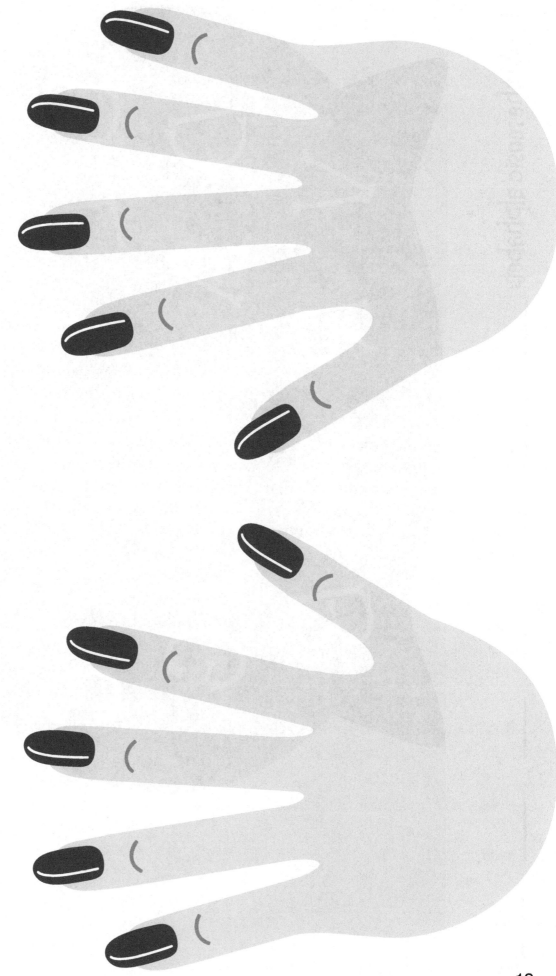

Music Alphabet Brew

Color the letters that do not belong
in the music alphabet black to make
them magically disappear!

Write the music alphabet: ___ ___ ___ ___ ___ ___ ___

B E P A Q C
D A F M G C
Y R H B

Sad Ghost or Happy Ghost?

For each music example, circle a happy ghost if it sounds happy, or circle the sad ghost if it sounds sad. Have a teacher or friend play these chords.

Up, Down, or Same?

Is the witch flying up, down, or staying the same? Circle the correct answer.

Up   Down   Same

Up   Down   Same

Up   Down   Same

Up   Down   Same

Up   Down   Same

Up   Down   Same

Up   Down   Same

Up   Down   Same

Up   Down   Same

Zombie Attack! No. 1

There's a wave of zombies on the move. Match them to the correct piano keys or they might come for you!

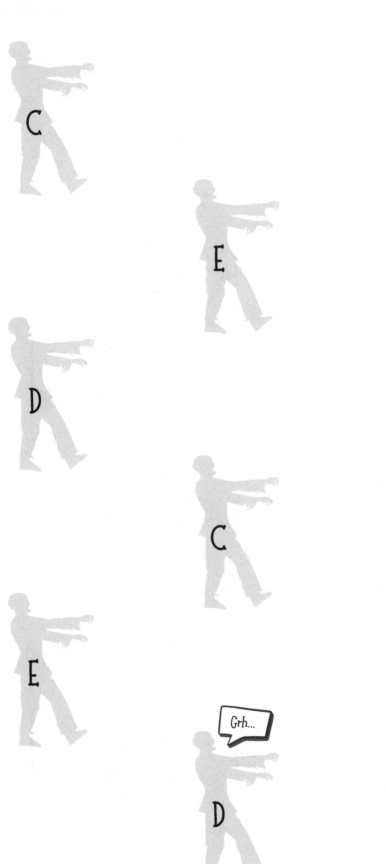

Count Dracula Rhythms No. 1

Match 'em up!

_____ Trick or Treat!

_____ They don't scare me!

_____ Booooo!

_____ Black cat

_____ Witch

_____ Howl! Howl!

A. 𝅝

B. ♩ ♩

C. ♩ ♩ ♩

D. ♩ ♩

E. ♩

F. ♩ ♩ ♩ ♩

18

Halloween Music Search

```
G  M  H  A  L  L  O  W  E  E  N  P
R  E  P  E  A  T  S  I  G  N  B  K
C  M  E  A  S  U  R  E  F  F  Q  S
A  B  N  R  S  M  P  I  A  N  O  T
N  O  O  F  O  R  T  E  D  B  A  A
D  O  T  T  C  O  S  T  U  M  E  F
Y  N  E  B  R  T  R  E  B  L  E  F
S  P  O  O  K  Y  B  A  S  S  J  E
```

Find the following words in the puzzle.
Words are hidden across and down.

MUSIC WORDS:
BASS
FORTE
MEASURE
NOTE
PIANO
REPEAT SIGN
STAFF
TREBLE

HALLOWEEN WORDS:
BOO
CANDY
COSTUME
HALLOWEEN
SPOOKY

Franken-stems

Add stems to the notes below.
Be careful not to create a Frankenstem!

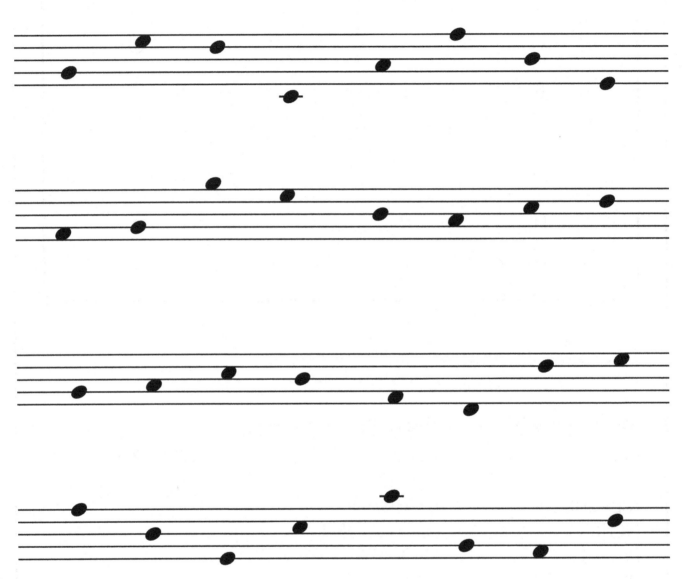

Color this Halloween scene by note using the color key below.

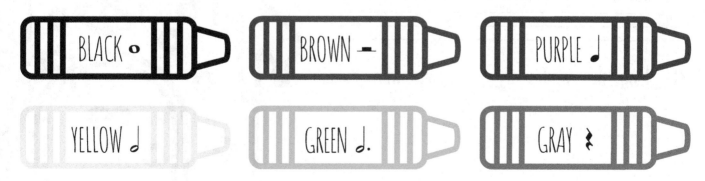

BLACK o   BROWN —   PURPLE ♩

YELLOW ♩   GREEN ♩.   GRAY 𝄽

21

The Scary Story of Hansel and Gretel

Hansel and Gr__t__l were __ brother and sister who __ot lost in the forest. Th__r__

they found a house m__ __ __ of gingerbread and c__n__y, so they knock__d

on the __oor. A witch opened the door and invit__ __ them in, but she w__nt__d

to f__tt__n them up and __ __t them! Gretel pushed the witch in the

ov__n, __nd the _rother and sister __s__ap__d while

t__king the witch's tr__ __sure with them.

Zombie Attack! No. 2

There's a wave of zombies on the move. Match them to the correct piano keys or they might come for you!

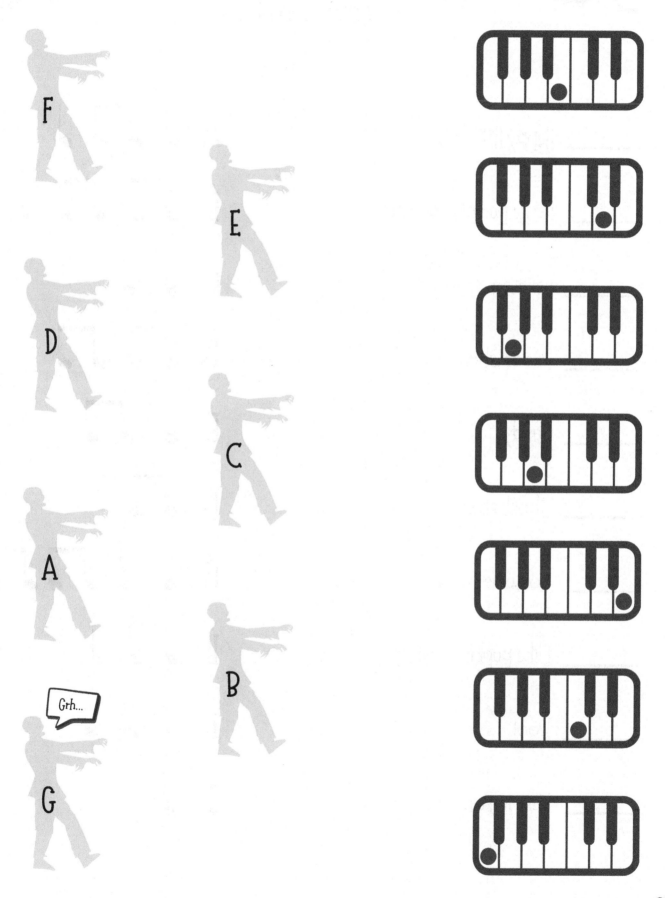

Count Dracula Rhythms No. 2
Match 'em up!

_____ Happy Halloween

_____ Large pumpkin patch

_____ Haunted house

_____ Broomstick

_____ Candy

_____ Ghost story

_____ Costume party

_____ I like pupkin carving!

_____ Boo!

_____ Rest in Peace

A.

B.

C.

D.

E.

F.

G.

H.

I.

J.

Supercharge My Broom

The witch is running late to a Halloween party. Help her get there quickly by circling all the tempo markings that mean fast.

Adagio

Largo

Vivace

Allegro

Lento

Grave

Prestissimo

Andante

Andantino

Moderato

Presto

Larghetto

Ghost Notes

Listen to the music examples on p. 75.
Fill in the missing notes to make the ghost notes appear.

Haunted Mansion Dynamics Maze

You've stumbled upon a haunted mansion to explore. Only pass through the halls that contain quiet dynamics (pp, p, or mp) or you might run into a monster!

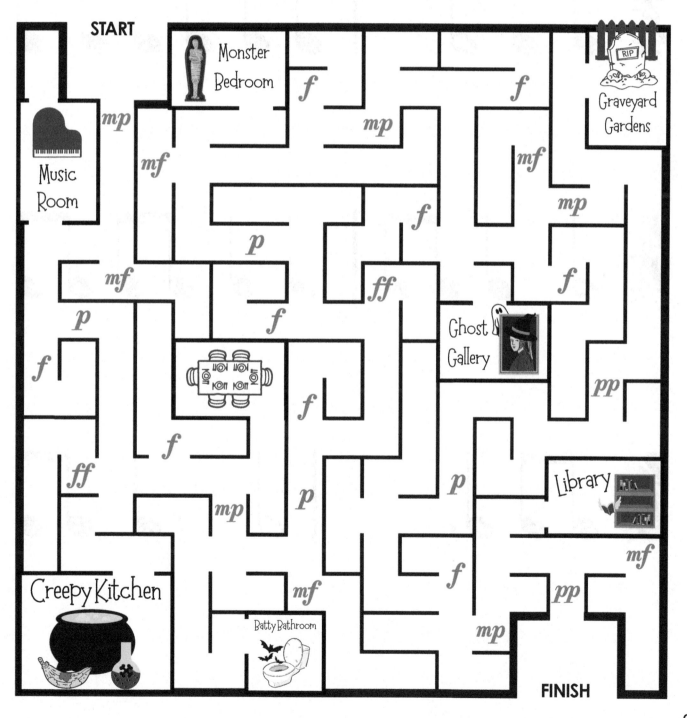

Count for Dracula

Dracula is confused and doesn't remember how to count rhythms.
Help him by writing in the counts under each note.
Then clap and count each rhythm.

Zombie Attack! No. 3

There's a wave of zombies on the move. Match them to the correct piano keys or they might come for you!

Match 'em up!

_____ Spooky

_____ Ghost

_____ Wicked witch

_____ Black cat

_____ Big Jack-o'-lantern

_____ Skeleton bones

_____ Really creepy

_____ Don't be a scaredy cat

_____ Boo to you!

_____ Count Dracula

A.

B.

C.

D.

E.

F.

G.

H.

I.

J.

Music and Monsters Search

```
E D W I T C H D A W G O S F S H N M
S P L V O L O Y B M R C L H P Q R E
H Z T I M E S I G N A T U R E M I Z
A D Y N A M I C S N Y A R F B U T Z
R B A S S C L E F Z X V J L C M A O
P Q Y S K E L E T O N E P A P M R F
E I G H T H N O T E E T M T Q Y D O
G A X W F R A N K E N S T E I N A R
G H O S T Y K V A M P I R E P J N T
G U M T R E B L E C L E F G B B D E
C R M E Z Z O P I A N O Q J Z J O W
O L E G A T O U R G Q A T P G F G I
```

Find the following words in the puzzle.
Words are hidden across and down.

MUSIC WORDS:
BASS CLEF
DYNAMICS
EIGHTH NOTE
FLAT
LEGATO
MEZZO FORTE
MEZZO PIANO
OCTAVE
RITARDANDO
SHARP
SLUR
TIME SIGNATURE
TREBLE CLEF

MONSTER WORDS:
FRANKENSTEIN
GHOST
MUMMY
SKELETON
VAMPIRE
WITCH

Musical Crossword

ACROSS

6. to gradually play slower

7. raises a note one half step

8. means loud

10. a note that gets one beat in $\frac{4}{4}$ time

11. means medium soft

12. the space between two bar lines

13. to play gradually louder

DOWN

1. the speed of music

2. lowers a note one half step

3. has five lines and four spaces

4. a pause on a note or rest

5. to play gradually softer

9. an interval of eight notes

Halloween Playlists

On the following pages, we've curated some great playlists for you to enjoy during the Halloween season. The lists are organized into three categories: classical, popular, and television/film. Search **Creative Piano Teacher** on YouTube to access the corresponding YouTube playlists.

Halloween Playlist Group Game Ideas

Pass the Prop: Using scarves, shakers, balls or whatever you choose, sit in a circle while the music plays and pass the object around the circle on the beat. Start off with the song's big beats and then try feeling smaller beats. Change directions to make it fun!

Freeze Dance: Show off your cool dance moves—but you have to freeze when the music stops! What fun dance pose did you end up in?

Musical Chairs: Play the music and have the players walk around a circle of chairs. There should be one chair less than the number of players participating. When the music stops, everyone must immediately sit in a chair. The one person left standing is out. Remove another chair and continue until only one person is left.

Name That Tune: Play the first 15 seconds of one of these familiar Halloween tunes. Can you name it?

Musical Charades: Write down the names of some halloween songs on slips of paper and put them in a container. When it's your turn, pull out one of the pieces of paper and act out the song title for others to guess. Play the song after you get it right!

Drumming: practicing playing with a steady beat on any kind of drum or homemade drums while you listen to the music.

Listening Activity Ideas

Musical Drawing: On a piece of paper, create a picture based on the lyrics of a song. This works for pieces without lyrics, too! Draw any image that comes to mind while listening.

Listening Worksheets: There are two listening prompt worksheets included in this book. These guided worksheets ask questions that will help you think about and understand the music you are listening to.

SP👻KY Classical Playlist

"Danse Macabre" by Saint-Saens

"The Water Goblin" by Antonin Dvorak

"Night on Bald Mountain" by Modest Mussorgsky

"Dream of a Witches' Sabbath" by Hector Berlioz

"Funeral March" by Frederic Chopin

"Totentanz Dance of the Dead" by Franz Liszt

"Toccata and Fugue in D Minor" by J. S. Bach

"Isle of the Dead" by Sergei Rachmaninoff

"Funeral March of the Marionette" by Charles Gounod

"In the Hall of the Mountain King" by Edvard Grieg

"With the Dead in a Dead Language" by Modest Mussorgsky

"The Witch" from Children's Album by Ilyich Tchaikovksy

"Suite from Psycho" by Bernard Herrmann

"Die Erlkonig" by Franz Schubert

"Inferno" from Dante Symphony by Franz Liszt

"O Fortuna" from Carmina Burana by Carl Orff

"Dies irae" from Messa da Requiem by Giuseppe Verdi

"The Sorcerer's Apprentice" by Paul Dukas

"The Banshee" by Henry Cowell

SPOOKY Popular Playlist

"The Skeleton in the Closet" by Louis Armstrong

"Thriller" by Michael Jackson

"Monster Mash" by Bobby Borris Pickett

"Spooky Scary Skeletons" by Andrew Gold

"Jeepers Creepers" by Paul Whiteman Orchestra

"The Cat Came Back" by Fred Penner

"Five Little Pumpkins" Traditional

"Purple People Eater" by Sheb Wooley

"I Put a Spell on You" by Screamin' Jay Hawkins

"Happy Halloween" by John Zacherle

"Monster Movie Ball" by Spike Jones

"Stop Look & Listen. It's Halloween" by Pete Antell

"Frankenstein Twist" by The Crystals

"Beat It" by Michael Jackson

"Sinister Stomp" by Bobby Boris Pickett

"Haunted House Blues" by Bessie Smith

"Zombie Jamboree" by Harry Belafonte

"Bogey Wail" by Jack Hylton

"Spooks" by Louis Armstrong

Halloween from The Screen Playlist

"Beetlejuice" from Beetlejuice

Halloween Theme

Ghostbusters Theme

"This is Halloween" from The Nightmare Before Christmas

"The Piano Duet" from The Corpse Bride

"The Great Pumpkin Waltz" from It's The Great Pumpkin Charlie Brown

"The Phantom of the Opera" from Phantom of the Opera

"Hedwig's Theme" from Harry Potter

The Addams Family Theme

The Munsters Theme

"Scooby Doo Where Are You?" from Scooby Doo the Movie

"Casper the Friendly Ghost" from Casper the Friendly Ghost

Dracula Theme (1979)

"Jack's Lament" from The Nightmare Before Christmas

"Grim Grinning Ghosts" from Disney's Haunted Mansion

"Poor Unfortunate Souls" from The Little Mermaid

Stranger Things Theme

"Time Warp" from The Rocky Horror Picture Show

"Rest in Peace" from Muppets Haunted Mansion

"Devil's Dance" from The Witches of Eastwick by John Williams

The Exorcist Theme

Dark Shadows Theme

The Twilight Zone Theme

Tales from the Crypt Theme

X-files Theme

Goosebumps Theme

Listening Prompt 1

1. Name of the piece you listened to:

_____

2. Which instruments/voices did you hear in this piece?

_____

3. Were the dynamics mostly loud, soft, or both?

_____

4. How did the music make you feel (scared, happy, sad, excited, etc)?

_____

_____

5. Was the speed of this piece mostly slow, medium, or fast?

_____

6. Did any sections repeat?   Yes   NO

7. What made this sound like Halloween music?

_____

_____

_____

_____

Listening Prompt 2

1. Name of the piece you listened to:

_____

2. Which instruments/voices did you hear in this piece?

_____

3. Were the dynamics mostly loud, soft, or both?

_____

4. How did the music make you feel (scared, happy, sad, excited, etc)?

_____

_____

5. Was the speed of this piece mostly slow, medium, or fast?

_____

6. Did any sections repeat?   Yes   NO

7. What made this sound like Halloween music?

_____

_____

_____

_____

_____

Listening Prompt 3

1. Name of the piece you listened to:

_____

2. Which instruments/voices did you hear in this piece?

_____

3. Were the dynamics mostly loud, soft, or both?

_____

4. How did the music make you feel (scared, happy, sad, excited, etc)?

_____

_____

5. Was the speed of this piece mostly slow, medium, or fast?

_____

6. Did any sections repeat?   Yes   NO

7. What made this sound like Halloween music?

_____

_____

_____

_____

Happy Halloween
Pre-staff Song

Davis Dorrough

Hap - py,   Hap - py   Hall - o - ween!   Cos - tumes come out   to   be   seen.
Get   a   trick   or   give   a   treat,   I'd   like   some - thing good   to   eat!

repeat

Hap - py,   Hap - py   Hall - o - ween!   How   I   love   the   spook - y   scene.

Watch   out   I   am   com - ing.   BOO!

40

A Scary Graveyard

Olivia Ellis

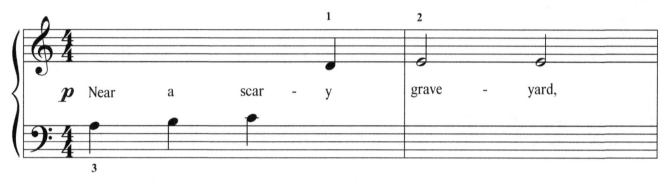

p Near   a   scar - y   grave - yard,

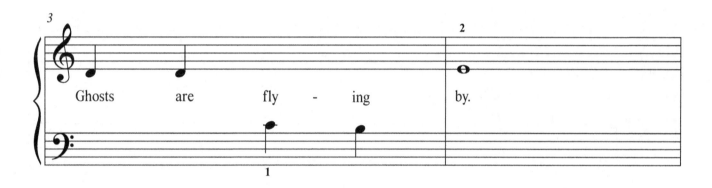

Ghosts   are   fly - ing   by.

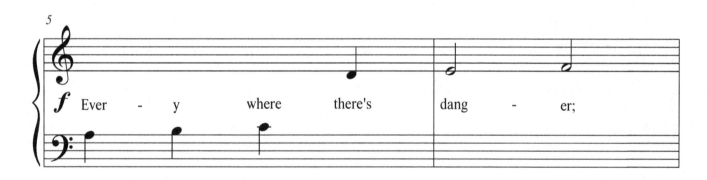

f Ev - y   where   there's   dang - er;

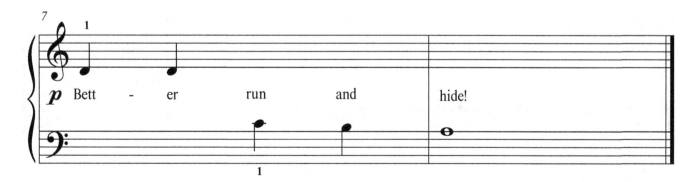

p Bett - er   run   and   hide!

A Boo-tiful Ghost

Davis Dorrough

p There is a boo - ti - ful ghost so fair,

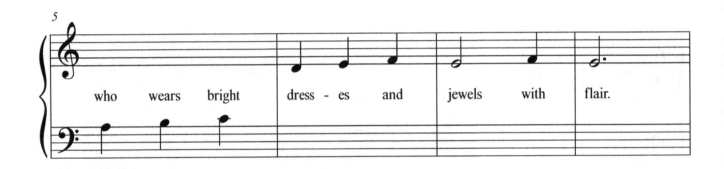

who wears bright dress - es and jewels with flair.

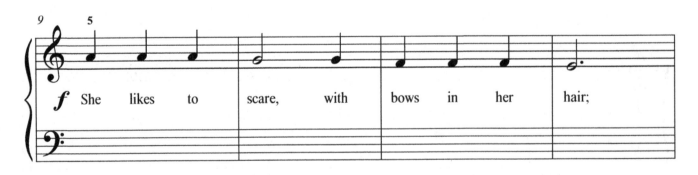

f She likes to scare, with bows in her hair;

highest A on piano

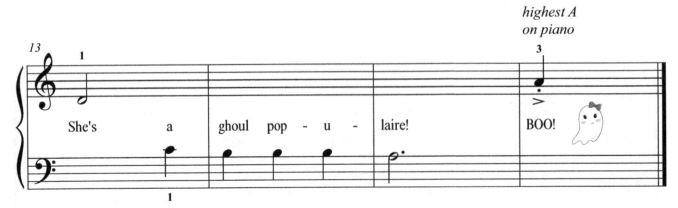

She's a ghoul pop - u - laire! BOO!

Trick or Treat on My Street

Olivia Ellis

Candy, Candy

Davis Dorrough

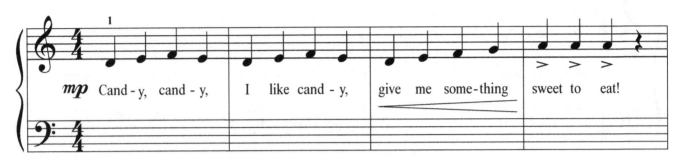

mp Cand - y, cand - y, | I like cand - y, | give me some-thing | sweet to eat!

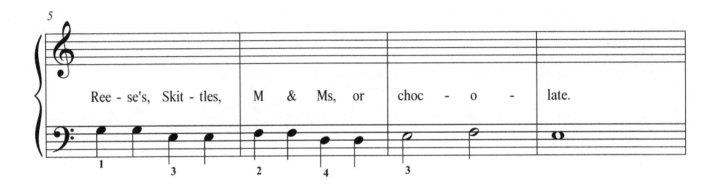

Ree - se's, Skit - tles, | M & Ms, or | choc - o - | late.

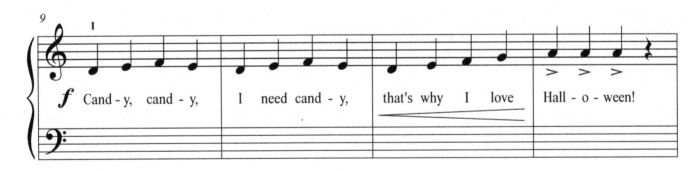

f Cand - y, cand - y, | I need cand - y, | that's why I love | Hall - o - ween!

Quick! Let's go and | trick or treat, it's | Hall - o - | ween.

Eight-Legged Creatures

Olivia Ellis

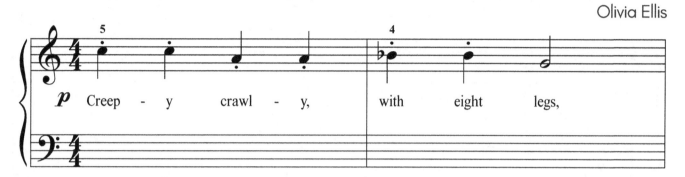

p Creep - y crawl - y, with eight legs,

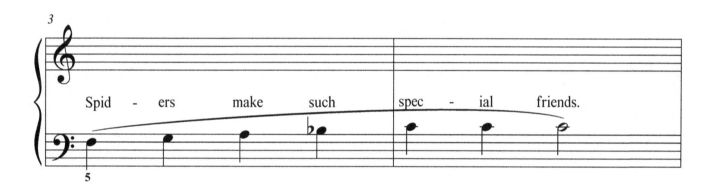

Spid - ers make such spec - ial friends.

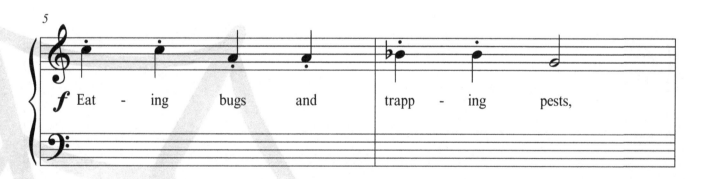

f Eat - ing bugs and trapp - ing pests,

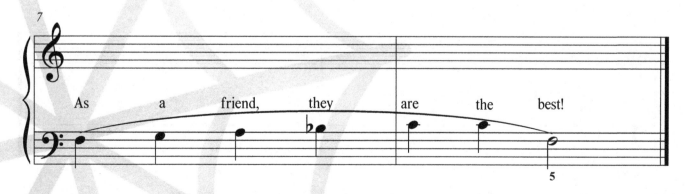

As a friend, they are the best!

45

Grumpy Old Ghost

Davis Dorrough

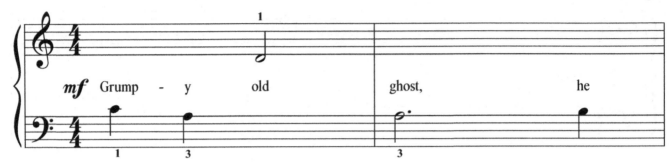

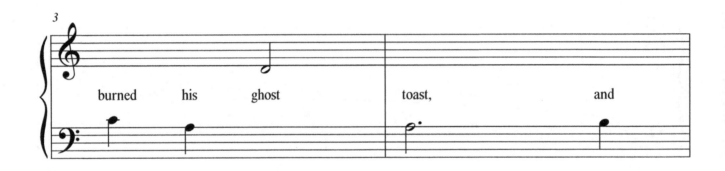

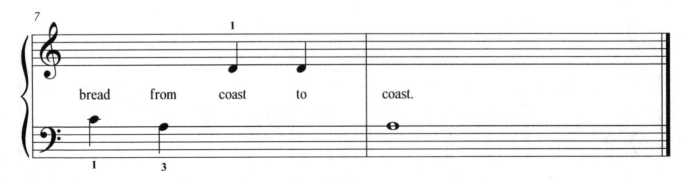

46

Jolly Jack-o'-Lanterns

Olivia Ellis

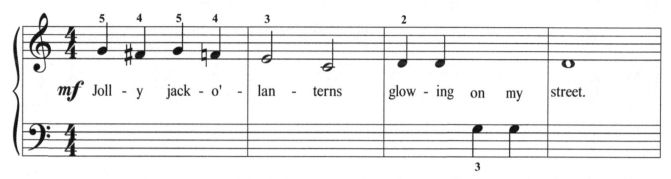

mf Joll - y jack - o' - lan - terns glow - ing on my street.

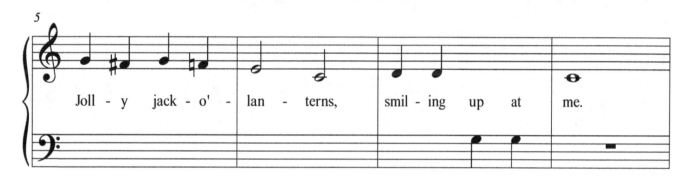

Joll - y jack - o' - lan - terns, smil - ing up at me.

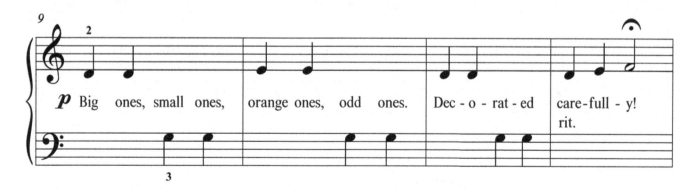

p Big ones, small ones, orange ones, odd ones. Dec - o - rat - ed care - full - y!
rit.

f Joll - y jack - o' - lan - terns, I want one for me!

The Monster Song

Davis Dorrough

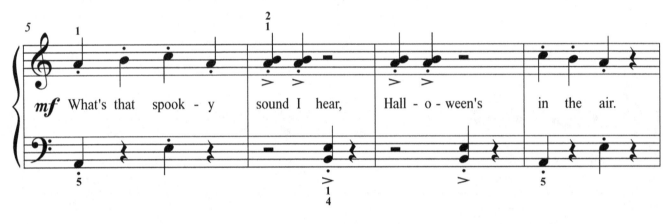

What's that spook - y sound I hear, Hall - o - ween's in the air.

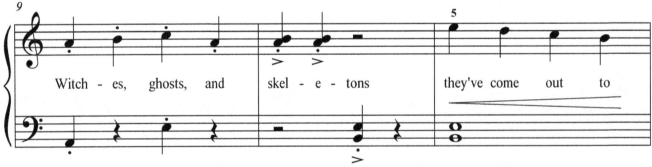

Witch - es, ghosts, and skel - e - tons they've come out to

scare! Drac - u - la, Frank - en - stein, they've ar - rived,

Black Cat Dance

Olivia Ellis

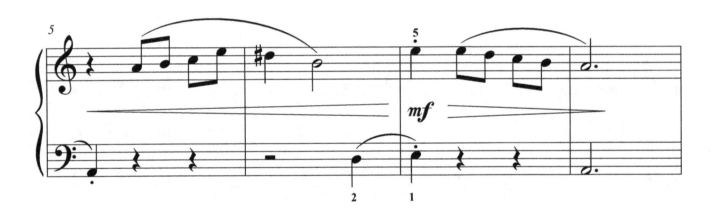

Black Cat Dance 2

Challenge Version

Olivia Ellis

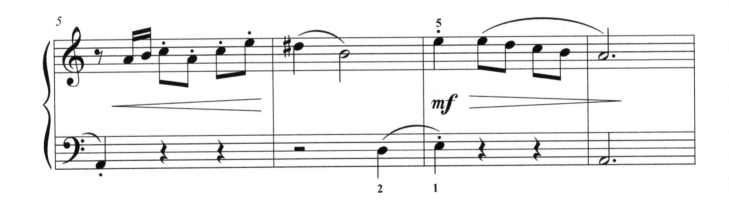

53

Creative Halloween Composing

On the following pages, we've provided some blank staff paper for creative Halloween composing. On this page, you'll find instructions and prompts to guide you.

Instructions

Title: On the top line, write your title.

Number of measures: A composition can be any number of measures. Try getting started with eight or sixteen measures and place two or four measures on each line. It creates a great structure for your first pieces.

Music symbols: Don't forget to draw the treble and bass clef, bar lines, and a double bar line at the end. Will your piece repeat? If so, include a repeat sign.

Form: Consider using AABA form. That means the first two lines will be similar, the third line different, and the fourth line similar to the beginning again. Then, try experimenting with different combinations.

Scale: Halloween music often has a dark, spooky sound. Consider using the first five notes of the A minor scale (A B C D E). Or, if you want a happy Halloween piece, use C D E F G.

Lyrics: If you want to write some haunting lyrics to go with your piece, place these between the treble and bass staves.

Simplify: Composing sometimes becomes overwhelming when we try to do too many different things and use too many notes. If you aren't sure where to start, just make a piece using two notes that are a half step apart! It will sound extra creepy!

Composition Topic Ideas

- Ghosts, skeletons, Frankenstein or any other Halloween characters

- Your favorite fall activities like pumpkin carving or trick-or-treating

- Haunted places like a haunted house, hotel, or graveyard

100 Halloween Words for Composing

afraid	creepy	Grim Reaper	nightmare	strange
alarming	crow	hair-raising	October	supernatural
apparition	crypt	Halloween	orange	superstition
autumn	dark	haunted	phantom	sweets
bat	darkness	haunted house	poltergeist	tarantula
bizarre	dead	hayride	potion	terrify
black	Dracula	hobgoblin	pumpkin	thirty-first
bones	eerie	horror	scary	thrilling
boo	fall	howl	scream	tombstone
broom	fangs	jack-o-lantern	shadowy	trick-or-treat
cackle	fog	lantern	shock	vampire
candle	Frankenstein	mask	shocking	vanish
candy	fright	masquerade	skeleton	wand
carve	frightening	midnight	skull	weird
cat	ghastly	monster	spell	werewolf
cauldron	ghost	moon	spider	wicked
cemetery	ghoul	moonlight	spiderwebs	wind
chilling	goblin	mummy	spine-chilling	witch
corpse	graveyard	mysterious	spirit	wizard
costume	grim	night	spooky	zombie

Cuttables

You'll notice there are several pages in the back of this book that are cuttables. These are meant to be cut out of the book and used for games, study cards, rhythm work, and more. Simply cut along the dotted lines and get ready for fun! We suggest laminating these if possible so you can keep them and reuse them over and over.

Ideas for Rhythm Pumpkins:

- Clap these rhythms to practice by yourself or in a group, moving up a level as you get better

- Create a melody on your instrument or by singing using the rhythms

- Clap the rhythm for a friend and see if they can clap it back

- Use this as a special challenge for earning prizes and party favors

Halloween Matching Game:

Mix up all the cards, then flip them over so you just see the decorative sides. Take turns flipping over two random cards to see if they match. If you get it right, tell the group what the music symbol means and then hang on to that match! If not, flip them back over. Try to remember where you spotted some of the musical Halloween characters so you can collect more. Whoever gets the most matches wins!

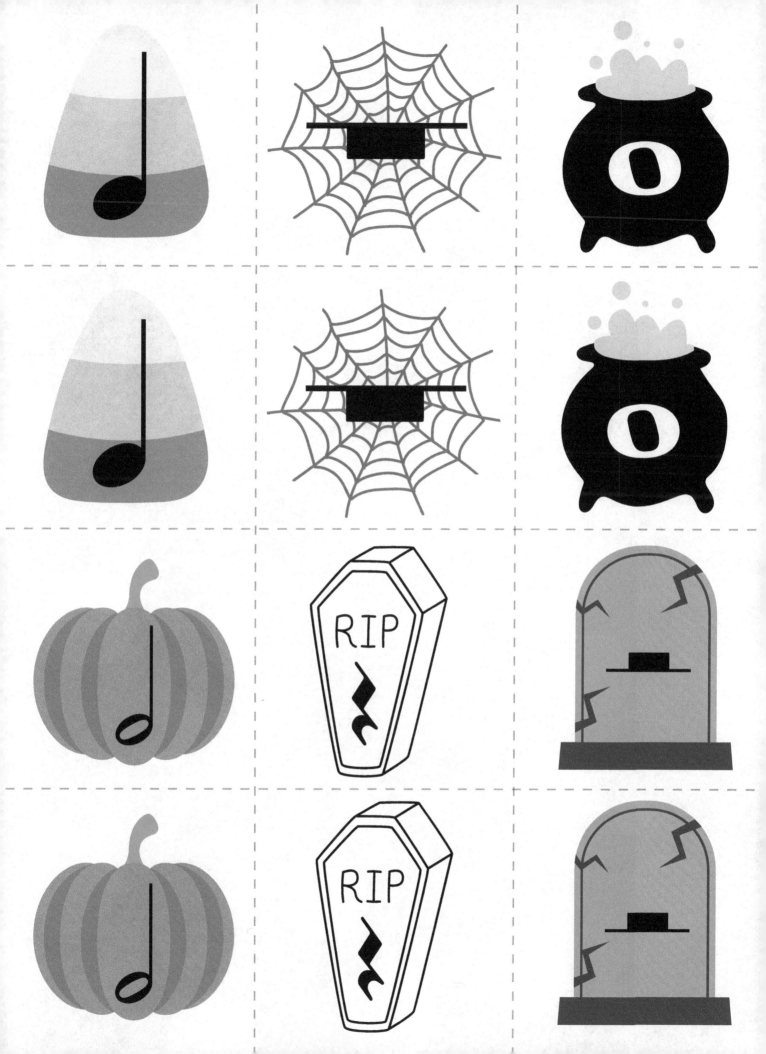

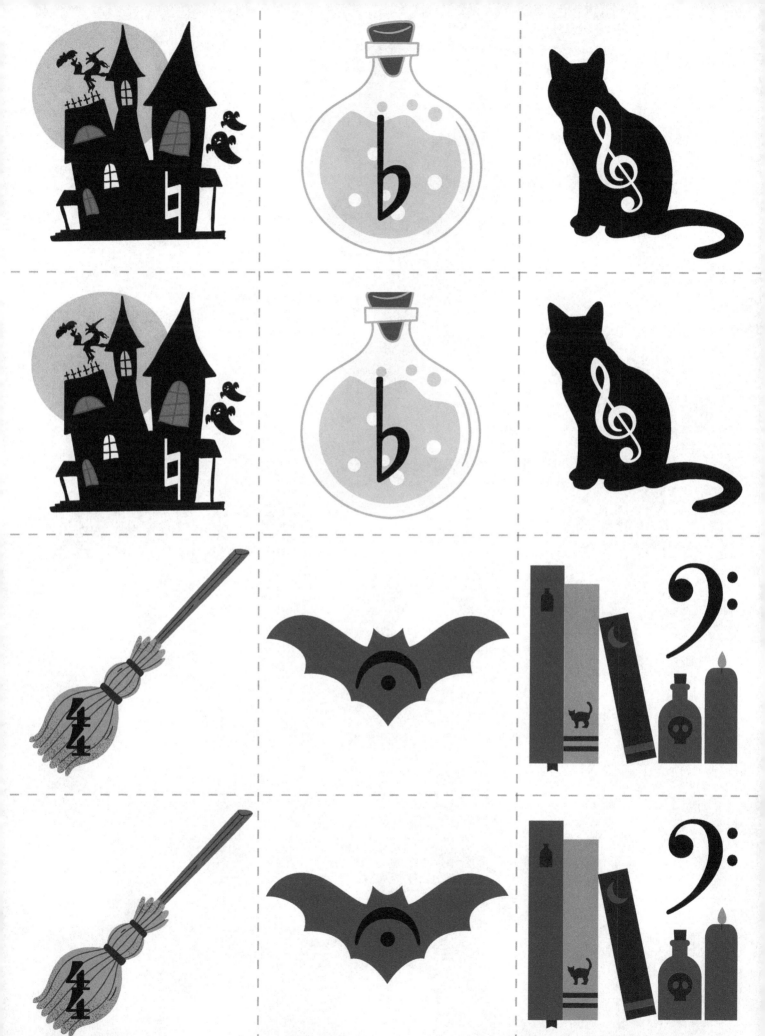

Ghost Notes Examples

Have someone play the following examples for the
Ghost Notes activity on p. 26.

Made in the USA
Coppell, TX
21 September 2024

37541048R20044